Evening Body

poems by

Karissa Knox Sorrell

Finishing Line Press
Georgetown, Kentucky

Evening Body

Copyright © 2016 by Karissa Knox Sorrell
ISBN 978-1-944251-38-3 First Edition
All rights reserved under International and Pan-American Copyright Conventions.
No part of this book may be reproduced in any manner whatsoever without written permission from the publisher, except in the case of brief quotations embodied in critical articles and reviews.

ACKNOWLEDGMENTS

"The Boulevard" and "Luminescence" *Gravel Magazine*, May 2015.
"Goddess Tree" and "Boneyard" *Alliterati Magazine*, Issue 6, January 2015.
"Chrysalis" *Silver Birch Press*, November 2014.
"Lobelia cardinalis" *Squawk Back*, Issue 129. 12 October 2014.
"Snowman" and "Evening Body" *Parable Press*, Quarterly Issue One. September 2013.
"Trains" *Cactus Heart*, Issue 3.5. May 2013.
"July Beans" *Flycatcher*, No. 2. January 2013.
"Miscarriage" *San Pedro River Review*, Spring 2011.
"Moon Garden" *Etchings*, Issue #9. March 2011.
"Microscopic" and "Notes to Sappho" *Number One*, Vol 38. 2010.
"Asking Vanessa about My Dead Brother Will" *Relief: A Christian Literary Expression*. Issue 3.2. 2009.

Editor: Christen Kincaid

Cover Art: Steven Sorrell

Author Photo: Karla Wardlow

Cover Design: Elizabeth Maines

Printed in the USA on acid-free paper.
Order online: www.finishinglinepress.com
also available on amazon.com

Author inquiries and mail orders:
Finishing Line Press
P. O. Box 1626
Georgetown, Kentucky 40324
U. S. A.

Table of Contents

Evening Body 1
Moon Garden 2
Mirrors 3
July Beans 4
Boneyard 5
Notes to Sappho 6
Snowman 8
Memory 9
Lobelia cardinalis 10
Goddess Tree 11
The Boulevard 12
Microscopic 13
Chrysalis 14
Trains 15
Seeds 16
Chores 17
Asking Vanessa about My Dead Brother Will 18
Ash 19
Exodus 20
Chasing the Heron 21
Miscarriage 22
Luminescence 23

for Steven

Evening Body

This is the way the trees
look at winter dusk: dark
capillaries poking the sky, mere
silhouette, the violet texture

of bark dissolved to black
skeletons of ash, ready to collapse
with the slightest breath.
This is when limbs suspend, hold

still in a moment of weakness.
Who doesn't wish for such
obscurity, the pink horizon bearing
the fragile body?

Moon Garden

Moths settle on the moonflower vine, waiting for
each bloom to open for its first and last time—one
night is all they get. Closed, the buds are a mass of swirls leading
toward a vortex. Then a star appears, the center
circle unravels into five points
hovering in the air. This is the most crucial
moment: will the bud open?

Although you are beside me, you cannot look at me.
Where is your glowing beauty, where is mine
in our tangled silence? Do you remember planting those seeds,
when you soaked them first, when I repainted
the old trellis, and all our roses died? How many times
have we planted,
and only this summer something finally grew?

Like a parachute, the flower
billows open in a burst,
receives the night into its white petals.
Fifty blooms ladder up the vine.

Mirrors

Needing no light, the basket star stretches
its branch-limbs searching the water, fingers
the coral for some delicacy. The vein-like clusters

of tentacles scrape the cold water until the star
extends, half a meter in diameter. It climbs
to a peak and embraces the current. Its arms

thwap against the surge, tendrils curl around
brine shrimp or the like, hooks snare the prey.
The creature feeds on the veiled depths.

        Far overhead, another kind of star burns
        in its own sea, its stellar wind streaming
        into space. Made by clouds of helium

        and hydrogen collapsing, now it
        holds in the balance between fusion and gravity.
        In a telescope its light dances, a trick of the rippling

        atmosphere. There is awe that comes
        looking upward, finding splinters of light
        that endure the mystery.

When day appears, the stars retreat. Those of us
in the space between don't know which way
to look: one star beyond our reach, the other
crossing floors of our shared earth.

July Beans

That was the summer the hummingbirds drank
Grandma out of Kool-Aid, everything ripening—
tomatoes plump, pink, cucumbers going yellow
and soft, green beans dangling on the trellis,
impatient as children. Grandma's cotton dress
waving at the knees, she sat me on the porch
with the pot between my knees, and I
tugged the thin strings down to snap
like threads of a hem, then breaking—ends first, then
middle. She came up once or twice to check on
me, rescuing a dozen poorly pulled beans
from the kettle and piling them back into my lap.
In the garden my grandmother filled two baskets:
one for the ripe things, another for the rotten,
and behind her the wind tried to help
white sheets escape the line.

Boneyard

> *If you find at your turn that none of the ends of your dominoes match, you must draw one domino from the boneyard.*
> —Mexican train rulebook

There is always a loss.

Overturned tiles
Smooth white sides beckoning
Click-clack of them touching
Each other, touching—

Which may not have existed for us, or if so,
I couldn't feel it
I could only know,
Know mentally, that you were with me

My Thai friend showed me a picture of her mother's
Ashes and bones.

Her son dug in the ashes with a shovel,
Throwing his grandmother around
Like sand in the box. I might have cringed, if I didn't know it as truth
already.

Loss is something we dig through
A weight that covers us
Buries us in misery, mystery, history,

An etymology that prefixes and suffixes
What we call love

Precipitates and *suffocates*, *paraphrases* and *sacrifices*, *piecemeals* and *scraps*

My turn comes
And goes, I choose
Dots unmatching

There are four polka-dotted trains, only one mine, and that
Opened by a penny, which means anyone can play on it.

I walk through the boneyard, fingering the stones, searching
For the ashes I scattered.

Notes to Sappho

I.

Would you find me in your fields,
lie with me in the balmy hands of the sun,
lap water from the stream, be alive
in a hush of reeds whose roots pierce the muddy banks?

II.

Today a poet does not wait for someone to listen.
She is buried in the leaves of everytree,
skin sweaty like any other human.

III.

The bee, drunk on nectar
from tickseed, pursues
the cricket, whose reedy trill
travels ageless wind.

IV.

Take me to the hill
to watch the sun shudder
the waters, confused with worries,
words that fall in rivers to drown.

V.

Which words were
fractured, burned, lost
in the knuckles of time?
Who will speak them
to me now?

VI.

Broken, the pen
lies upon yellow
leaves beneath us,
the last leaf a farewell
to fall, the maple
bare and proud.

VII.

Help me gather the lines
between us, hang them
over the old moon,
its glowing patina
that never tires
of illuminating.

Snowman

Listen is a make-believe word,
a translation cut up by the heave
of talk. You said it, and I watched
the robin puffed up in his nest.
You said, but I poured milk
in snow.

The garbage truck man interpreted
my scream with a wave, screech
of wet brakes. You said, not in
front of the neighbors, but wasn't
it too late?

If not you, the snowman, then, forcing
the carrot into his face. Saying is all-
knowing in disguise. There is always
another word.

If I were a bird,
would I fly?

Memory

The dream ended.

Wake up. Unravel.

Was it a road, or was it the flying
of your satin ribbon across the air—
so close to my face, a darkness
almost pierced by your silhouette.

The mind passes through the brain,
travels the path of electric impulses
down nerves and across synaptic
gaps, looking for a place to land.

Will it land beside you, wherever
that might be, in a field of primroses
over the cerebellum, some sort of
heaven in clouds of blood, or your
face tilted toward mine in a memory?

No.

I am back at the road
on which I am always walking,
all the world unknotting around me,
even the dreams coming undone at
the wayside, knowing that
I won't find you.

Lobelia cardinalis

Late afternoon.

Five miles around and up Gregory's Bald
in mid-October drizzle. The mud squishes
under our shoes, earthworms squirming,
acorns and animal pellets drowning.

I crouch to fix an untied boot;
when I stand up, you are gone.
I'm alone with just
the whisper of rain touching leaves.

The trail bleeds into a slope clumped
with brush and trees; should I try to follow it,
hoping to find you again?

Or should I turn back, plunge across
that swelling creek and down the muddy
mountainside, steadying myself with
drenched birch branches?

The day has drifted between us
like a veil of petals falling
from the cardinal flower.

As evening approaches, I disappear
into the shadows, upwards into the tangled
landscape that waits.

Goddess Tree

You cannot be a goddess
they told me, because
*we can't have a woman
parading and pretending*

So I let all the men
plant their seed inside me
and I birthed
the most lovely flower
that opened to every sunrise

Then that flower became
a fruit, which I picked
and ate down to the core
while they watched the juices
skiing down my chin

When I came to the seed
I ate it, too, and it grew in me
until my human torso
was covered in bark
my legs and toes morphed into roots
and my arms stiffened
into strong, heavy branches

People flocked to me
for my shade,
my fruit, and some said
they could hear
a song
when they pressed
their ear
against me.

The Boulevard
(A Found Poem)

Even his parents left everything free
to watch endless nature trails
found on corkboards for which the sea is now turning.
Entering from the rear door,
the silence between one Rome and another, conducive
for love, for drinks, more drinks. The perimeters are open
for us to meet unique trees, cut by sunrays and more
competitive sunrays. We find a fish on the disc
golf course, a small exhibit, a life drawing, a revision
of caution. On the boulevard, we lean together
over cups of tea.

Microscopic

While Mom and Dad
watched a man walk
on the moon, I wiped
sweat from my face and tried,
for the seventh time,
to see the atoms
in my torn-off fingernail.
It was the microscope
Dad gave me that I turned to
every time. Catching
a wasp, I placed it
beneath the lens and
thought I felt its stinger
in my eye.

Like that wasp, tonight
the stars appear
to sting, though
they are already dead.
This fear was why
I loved that microscope,
why I loved my father, even
when he didn't see me.

On the stargazing rock,
my son takes his
turn at the eyepiece,
points of light aligning
into invented constellations:
cloud, robot, bird.
In the telescope the radiance
springs toward us. My son
takes my hand,
the distance erased.

Chrysalis

I am waiting for a god I can touch.
I am waiting to feel the world turning,
to sense myself moving at a thousand
miles an hour. I am waiting to shout
to the universe *I am here!* To hope that
something out there is silent enough
to hear me. I am waiting to birth
a voice that echoes.

I am waiting for another I am,
for the incense of burning bush
on the air, for something I might recognize
as miracle, which might be as
quiet as a naked branch in winter
or my son's heartbeat beneath my fingers.

I am waiting for the stars
to explain themselves instead
of disappearing into the past.
I am waiting for the earth
to rise up and claim itself
away from us. I am waiting for
an earthquake to split the chrysalis
wide open until every tethered
winged thing breaks into flight.

Trains

Lips press on panes, breath
fogging, fingertips mist and smudge.
Spoons click, stirring the cream, lean
against the edge of the cup. The heat
is too much. Shoes nudge into the aisle,
an elbow or two. Books thump closed,
unloved. Cover the cold night in sleep.
This, so you don't know what happens.

> I unload; you load. Until the day
> that you just don't anymore. The tank
> fills and empties and fills again. Thank
> you abandons us. The wash lies still
> wet in the dryer, forgotten. A drain
> clogs, but we just move to another sink.

Brakes scream, wail of metal cracking
the air where forks fall upward, scrape
the place a window used to be. Shards of glass
stick in skin, suitcases fly. A blanket
free-falls, comes to rest on wet grass.
A spark, a light, heat ignites. Fire burns
into the freezing air, licks the broken
metal cars. No one knows why.

> There are only two bodies here; yours and mine.
> Neither is moving. We lie here quietly,
> counting our wounds, counting our slowing
> heartbeats.

Seeds

> *"I now knew that when the great guiding spirit cleaves humanity into two antagonistic halves, I will be with the people."*
> —*Ernesto Che Guevara*

We rib the continent and watch
its seams split, feel its frigid air creep
over our skin, freeze our blood
into suspended droplets we hand
to the Pachamama.

Nights, I call to her and ask her to plant
the blood-seeds into the soil of this land,
let it soak and soak
until the skins of all the plants and animals
and humans belong to it,

one bloodline
forged from the drops that will trickle
down my face when I rise up
to reclaim this splintering body.

For now we tremble in the cold
face of night on the mountain,
suffering side by side
with our indian brothers.

And I wait for my time to come.

Chores

At the kitchen counter,
knife gleaming in my fist,
brown dust coming off on my hands,
potato skin like damp cardboard,
making the first cut too deep,
cutting out the flesh we were
supposed to eat, dumping thick
layers of skin and tissue into
the sink, the blackened pot
mounding with white jagged
slices spotted red from
nicks and cuts in my fingers, which
Mama cleaned and bandaged only
after she'd rinsed
the potatoes of blood.

Asking Vanessa about My Dead Brother Will

What did you say, Vanessa, when you heard he'd died?
I cried, and I remembered
Remembered what?
Eastern sun illuminating our porcelain faces, dolls handled
by children who so easily discard love
And when you left that place, what did he say to you?
He asked me to wait for him.
And why didn't you?
After he died, I waited for him, and he came to me in a dream.
What did he tell you?
The travel of ships between lands relies
on the heavens and the spirits. We meet at the places
between, over the waters.

I said to him
what needs to be said?
Before he died, he asked for you.
How long did it take him to die?
About four hours. He suffered from the
head injury, groaned your name, reached
for a comfort too far away.
Where did you bury him?
In the sea, beside his home.
A cemetery of predators, why would you leave him there?
He waits for you with the waters, he waits for you to sail to him.
Why did it take you so long to find me?
I wanted to leave him dead, but I thought
Did you think I loved him?
I know you did once.
Will I find him again?
His spirit roves our old land
By the sea
By the sea.

Ash

A fire is spreading through my house,
turning all the furniture black. The four-poster bed

we loved each other in has already collapsed,
the teddy bears on the shelf have turned to smoke

and fuzz. A man walks into the room—it must be you—
you are carrying the children, one under each arm.

You speak, and the oxygen laced in your breath
feeds the flames, propelling them

toward the kitchen cabinets. I can't hear
your words, and the fire keeps burning.

Now the flames are crawling over the photographs,
snaking into the office. They climb up the legs

of the desk and devour every scrap of paper—
the children's coloring, a grocery list,

English tests, a poem. I follow the blaze,
covering my mouth but keeping my eyes open.

Through the sting I watch tongues
of fire attack the bookcases.

All the books are burning,

all my words: they blaze, they ash.

Exodus

The migrants flex their wings, prepare to make
an unknown journey. Their farthest move
      has been mere miles. Across a continent
      the wind will bear the fourth generation,

          the grass like seaweed draping sand castles,
           lakes, dark like night, glitter with sunlight stars,
all views are skewed by height, by hope.
A child first spies their advent, a simultaneous

descent of spirits of the ancestors
on Mexico's Day of the Dead. Butterflies
      cascade into this holiday each year,
      triumphant, expected. What force guided

          them here—something innate, or something more
          like fate? The monarch migrants disregard
this mystery; as fireworks proclaim,
bright wings whisper like rain and swathe the trees.

Chasing the Heron

Running around the man-made lake
the great blue heron
at the water's edge
surprised me. Why
take shelter in a neighborhood
loud with dog barks
and bulldozers?

Each time my
shoes and heavy breath
clunked near
the heron startled and flew
across the water, its wingspan
endless in mid-air,
neck folded into an s.

That s might have been
a river it once called home
or the way my body curls
into bed at night or a scar
along my calf.

Those rippled wings might
tell a story of the need
to find a place
to call one's own
or maybe the need
to call yourself
worthy
of the place you inhabit.

Again, I would pass, again
the hard whisper of wings,
the ever flight toward
elsewhere, never being able
to stay.

Miscarriage

When the doctor's visit is over the husband
whispers and you know something
has been lost. There was a moment

      heart startled and released
the hushed sound that marks a grief. A grave
is not needed for this. But a mother

wants a place for her child. That echo
coats branches like a light snow
tapping all the way down your window.

            Stroke, stroke of the hawk's
wings far above. When the beating
stops, a prayer billows up.

The mother, the only one
who came close to the baby,
lets go of silence.

Luminescence

Inside the body of the world
there lives a vine
that awakens
in footprints and rootprints,

that touches our suffering

that heals the broken earth

that intertwines our pulses

until our breaths carry a new seed

within them.

While we sleep rain saturates the land
and in the morning
a luminescence
tunnels through fog.

I want to be the world, freshly washed.

Karissa Knox Sorrell is a writer, poet, and educator from Nashville, Tennessee. She earned her MFA from Murray State University in 2010. Her poetry and nonfiction have been seen in a variety of journals and magazines, including *St. Katherine Review, Parable Press, Etchings, Rock & Sling, Flycatcher, Relief Journal, Cactus Heart, Silver Birch Press,* and *San Pedro River Review*. She also has an essay in a forthcoming anthology titled *Soul Bare: Raw Stories of Human Redemption*. In addition to writing poetry, Karissa is currently working on a YA novel.

Karissa also has a fifteen-year career in education. After teaching K-12 ESL for eleven years, she now works as an instructional coach for the Office of English Learners of Metro Nashville Public Schools. She trains and mentors teachers who work with ESL students.

Karissa lives with her husband and two children in Nashville, Tennessee. Together they enjoy hiking, reading, theater, and spending time with family and friends.

www.ingramcontent.com/pod-product-compliance
Lightning Source LLC
Chambersburg PA
CBHW051706040426
42446CB00009B/1326